NORTH AMERICAN WILDLIFE

SKUNKS

by Joanne Mattern

Kaleidoscope
Minneapolis, MN

The Quest for Discovery Never Ends

This edition first published in 2024 by Kaleidoscope Publishing, Inc.

*For information regarding permission, write to
Kaleidoscope Publishing, Inc.
6012 Blue Circle Drive
Minnetonka, MN 55343*

*Library of Congress Control Number
2023936937*

*ISBN
978-1-64519-731-7 (library bound)
978-1-64519-779-9 (ebook)*

Printed in the United States of America.

Bigfoot lurks within one of the images in this book. It's up to you to find him!

TABLE OF CONTENTS

Chapter 1

WHAT'S THAT SMELL?

It is nighttime. A skunk moves through the darkness. It is looking for food. The skunk digs tiny insects called **grubs** out of the ground. There are plenty of grubs to make a tasty meal.

Suddenly, the skunk hears a noise. It looks up. A coyote is creeping through the tall grass. The skunk knows that danger is approaching. Coyotes are **predators**, and the skunk is about to be its **prey**. However, the skunk has a few tricks to play.

Skunks are not good at fighting. But they are very good at defending themselves. This skunk is about to scare away its enemy.

First, the skunk hisses. It is telling the coyote, "Stay away from me!" But the coyote does not listen. It moves closer.

Next, the skunk stomps its feet. It is warning the coyote to leave it alone. But the coyote does not care. No matter how much the skunk stomps, the coyote keeps coming.

The skunk turns its back end toward the coyote. It raises its tail high in the air. This is the coyote's last warning. Something bad is about to happen!

Finally, the coyote gets too close. It's time for the skunk to release its hidden weapon.

FUN FACT
There are four different species of skunks.

The skunk sprays a stinky liquid from **glands** under its tail. The spray smells really, really bad. The coyote jumps back. Then it runs away. This predator may be bigger and tougher than a little skunk. But there is no way it wants to eat this smelly animal for dinner!

The skunk goes back to digging up grubs. But the bad smell stays in the air for a long time.

SICKENING BUT NOT POISONOUS

A skunk's spray smells really bad. It can make a person's eyes water. It can even make them throw up. But a skunk's spray is not poisonous. It does not harm people or animals.

Chapter 2

A SKUNK'S BODY

The common striped skunk lives all over North America. It is about the size of a large house cat. A skunk is about 18 to 32 inches (46–81 cm) long. It weighs about 13 pounds (5.9 kg).

FUN FACT

Some other species of skunks look a little different. The spotted skunk has white spots all over its black fur.

Skunks are very easy to identify. This animal is covered with black fur. A white stripe runs down each side of its back. The stripes meet at the animal's tail, which is also white. The stripes make the skunk easy to see, even in the dark. It also has a bar of white fur between its eyes.

A skunk has a small head and a pointy face. It has short, strong legs. Skunks move slowly. They cannot run fast. Many skunks are hit by cars because they do not run away from danger. Instead, they stand still.

A skunk's feet have long, sharp claws. These claws are great for digging. Skunks also use their claws to fight each other.

A skunk's tail is long and **bushy**. It usually carries its tail down low. If a skunk raises its tail, look out! It is probably about to spray.

A skunk has two glands under its tail. The skunk can spray its smelly liquid out of these glands. A skunk has very good aim. If a predator is too close, the skunk will spray the liquid right in its eyes. If the predator is farther away, the spray can hang in the air. No animal wants to run through that to catch the skunk!

A STRONG SMELL

A skunk's spray can be smelled up to a mile and a half (2.4 km) away. A skunk can spray more than 10 feet (3.0 m). It can spray five or six times before its glands are empty. In about 10 days, they will fill up with more stinky liquid.

Chapter 3

A SKUNK'S LIFE

A mother skunk takes care of her babies by herself. She will build a den in a safe space. Skunks will den inside a hollow log, under some rocks, or under a building. Sometimes they find an old woodchuck **burrow** to live in.

Baby skunks can make their scent when they are born. But it takes about four months for them to spray on-target.

Four to six babies, or kits, are born in late spring. The babies stay with their mother for about eight weeks. She nurses them and keeps them safe.

When the kits are eight weeks old, they are able to find food and keep themselves safe. But they stay with their mother for about one year.

Skunks are **omnivores**. They eat many different things. These animals are **nocturnal**. They are active at night. Skunks love to dig up grubs and other insects. They eat mice and frogs. They eat bird eggs, berries, and mushrooms too. Corn on the cob tastes good, and so does honey from beehives.

Skunks even eat snakes. A snake's venom does not affect a skunk. So, it can even kill and eat a rattlesnake!

Skunks will also eat garbage. A skunk can't open a garbage can by itself. But sometimes it finds trash left by a raccoon or bear. It will look for food scraps to eat.

Skunks live in almost every **habitat**. They live in fields, woods, and swamps. They live near people in towns and cities.

It's easy to tell if a skunk is in your neighborhood. You will probably smell it. You can also see their tracks in mud or snow. Skunks have five toes with a claw on each one.

MAKING NOISE

Skunks are usually very quiet. But these animals can be loud if they want to. A skunk can hiss and screech. It can whimper or growl. These sounds are ways for skunks to communicate.

Where Do SKUNKS Live?

Chapter 4

SAVING SKUNKS

Skunks live only two to three years in the wild. These animals face many dangers. They are good at spraying coyotes and other land predators. But it's hard for a skunk to stay safe from danger in the sky. Birds of prey, such as eagles and hawks, often dive down and grab skunks. Baby skunks are especially in danger from these animals.

Skunks can also catch serious diseases. Some skunks catch **rabies**. This disease makes the skunk so sick it dies. If you see a skunk during the day, or a skunk that acts sick or **aggressive**, do not go near it. Call the police for help.

Like most wild animals, skunks are losing their homes. People cut down trees and dig up fields. They build roads, homes, and structures. There are fewer wild places where skunks can live.

Luckily, skunks can live almost anywhere. They eat many different things, so it is easy for them to find food. Their stinky smell keeps people and predators away. Skunks live in cities and parks. One might even live in your backyard!

People are not always happy when a skunk moves in. These animals are smelly. They dig up lawns. They can carry diseases that make people and pets sick.

Some people keep skunks as pets! Pet skunks have their scent glands removed.

Skunks can cause problems. But they can also be good neighbors. Skunks eat many insect pests. Some farmers like to have skunks around because they protect crops from damage.

The best way to get along with a skunk is to leave it alone. If you see a skunk, do not go near it. Walk away slowly in a different direction. Do not let your pets, especially dogs, near a skunk. Otherwise, you will all need a very good bath!

SWEET PERFUME?

Believe it or not, skunk spray is used in perfume! A skunk's spray includes several chemicals. Some of these chemicals are added to perfumes to make the scent last longer.

BEYOND THE BOOK

After reading the book, it's time to think about what you learned. Try the following exercises to jump-start your ideas.

THINK

LEARN ABOUT SKUNKS. There are several different kinds of skunks. Go to the library or on the Internet to find information about each kind. Where do they live? What do they look like? Write an article or make a poster featuring fun facts about different skunks and their homes.

CREATE

MAKE A SKUNK MASK. Look up pictures of skunks. Then draw or paint your own skunk mask. Share your work with your family and friends.

SHARE

THE MORE YOU KNOW. Share what you have learned about skunks with your classmates and friends. What are the main ideas in this book? What makes skunks special? Write a report or present a short video to share information.

GROW

MEET A SKUNK! While you don't want to meet a skunk in your neighborhood, there are safe ways to get to know these animals. Find out if a nearby zoo or wildlife museum has a skunk. Or get a long-distance view by searching up videos on the Internet.

RESEARCH NINJA

Visit www.ninjaresearcher.com/7317 to learn how to take your research skills and book report writing to the next level!

Research

DIGITAL LITERACY TOOLS

SEARCH LIKE A PRO
Learn how to use search engines to find useful websites.

FACT OR FAKE
Discover how you can tell a trusted website from an untrustworthy resource.

TEXT DETECTIVE
Explore how to zero in on the information you need most.

SHOW YOUR WORK
Research responsibly—learn how to cite sources.

Write

DOWNLOADABLE BOOK REPORT FORMS

GET TO THE POINT
Learn how to express your main ideas.

PLAN OF ATTACK
Learn prewriting exercises and create an outline.

Further Resources

BOOKS

Caswell, Deanna. *Baby Skunks*. Mankato, MN: Black Rabbit Books, 2020.

Klatte, Kathleen A. *Skunks at Night*. New York: PowerKids Press, 2020.

McDonald, Amy. *Skunks*. Minneapolis, MN: Bellwether Media, 2022.

WEBSITES

FACTSURFER

Factsurfer.com gives you a safe, fun way to find more information.

1. Go to www.factsurfer.com.
2. Enter "Skunks" into the search box and click 🔍
3. Select your book cover to see a list of related websites.

Glossary

aggressive: Ready to attack

burrow: An underground home for an animal

bushy: Thick like a bush

glands: Organs that release chemicals

grubs: Insect larvae that live underground

habitat: A place where an animal or plant is usually found

nocturnal: Active at night

omnivores: Animals that eat both plants and animals

predators: Animals that hunt and eat other animals

prey: An animal hunted by another animal

rabies: A contagious and fatal disease spread by mammals

species: One of the groups into which animals and plants of the same genus are divided

About the Author

Joanne Mattern is the author of hundreds of children's nonfiction books. Her favorite topics include science, animals, sports, history, and biography. Joanne lives in New York State with her husband and family.

Index

PHOTO CREDITS

The images in this book are reproduced through the courtesy of: Geoffrey Kuchera/Shutterstock Images, cover; Nynke van Holten/Shutterstock Images, p. 3; James Opiyo/Shutterstock Images, p. 4; Karel Bock/Shutterstock Images, p. 4–5; Brenda Carson/Shutterstock Images, p. 6; National Park Service/Wikimedia Commons, p. 7; Fiona M. Donnelly/Shutterstock Images, p. 8; Agnieszka Bacal/Shutterstock Images, p. 9; Geoffrey Kuchera/Shutterstock Images, p. 11; Yasmins world/Shutterstock Images, p. 12; yhelfman/Shutterstock Images, p. 13; Eric Isselee/Shutterstock Images, p. 14; Andrea Mazzei/Shutterstock Images, p. 15; Betty Shelton/Shutterstock Images, p. 16; Shutterstock Images, p. 17; Delovely Pics/Shutterstock Images, p. 18; Geoffrey Kuchera/Shutterstock Images, p. 19; Adwo/Shutterstock Images, p. 20; critterbiz/Shutterstock Images, p. 22; otsphoto/Shutterstock Images, p. 23; Images Azzaro/Shutterstock Images, p. 24–25; Frank Fichtmueller/Shutterstock Images, p. 26; Freebird7977/Shutterstock Images, p. 27; Nynke van Holten/Shutterstock Images, p. 31.